M. Evans and Company
titles are distributed in the United States
by the J. B. Lippincott Company,
East Washington Square
Philadelphia, Pa. 19105,
and in Canada by McClelland & Stewart Ltd.,
25 Hollinger Road, Toronto M4B 3G2, Ontario

Library of Congress Catalog Card No. 77-24416
ISBN 0-87131-238-7
Manufactured in the United States of America

DEDICATED

to the five men who _definitely_ made a billion dollars

1978551

ROCKEFELLER · MELLON · FORD · GETTY · HUGHES

(and to the handful of other rascals who _probably_ did, but were slick enough to keep it a secret.)

A BILLION

Now, that's a really

OOLLARS!

nice piece of change!

A billion is a
thousand million,
or a thousand-
thousand-thousand.
dollars.

It's a very comfortable
sum.

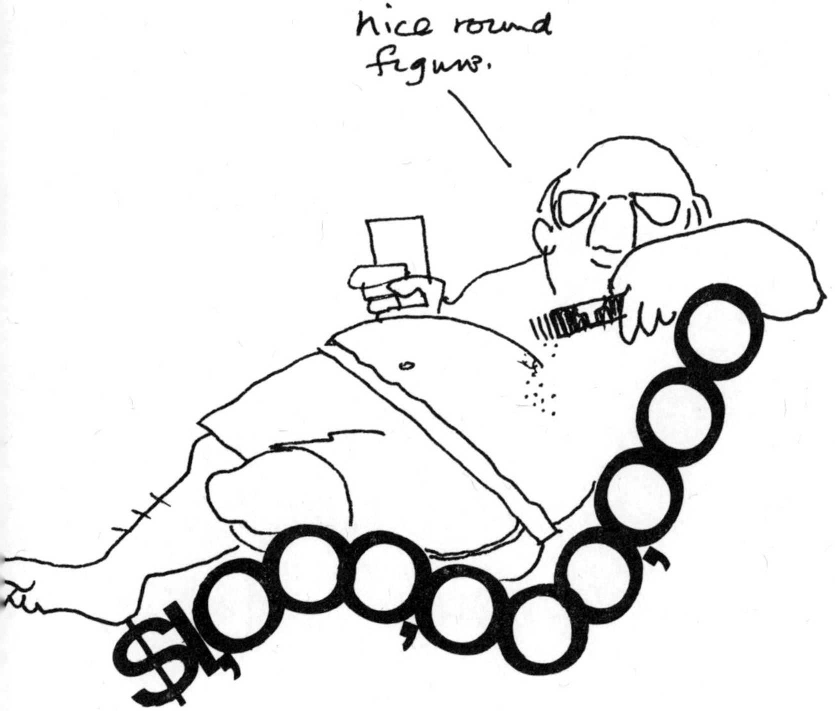
nice round figures.
$1,000,000,000

And the best part is,
they keep cranking
'em out. Every two-and-
a-half weeks, the
Bureau of Printing
and Engraving
prints, cuts, bands
and distributes
another billion dollars.

A billion dollars uses up a lot of paper. Enough to print two million copies of the Gideon Bible.

Holy cashflow!

That's enough paper to pave Pacific Highway No. One

with dollar bills
from San Francisco
to L.A.*

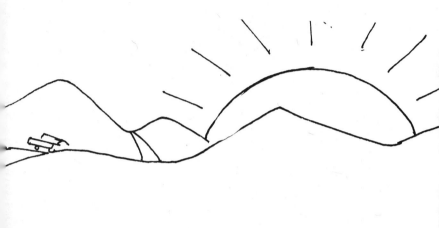

* with $81 million
left over for
walking-around money
when you get there.

Just for the record
a billion dollars
would also make a
ribbon reaching
four times around
the earth. (For
some reason,
people always
want to know

how far things
will go around
the earth.)

Simply finding a place to put a billion dollars poses problems.

A stack of them would reach over 69 miles high.

A billion dollars weigh
as much as an infant

...ivision — 2,500,000 pounds.

...nd that's just PAPER dollars...

A billion
silver dollars
weighs more than
the entire population
of Nevada.

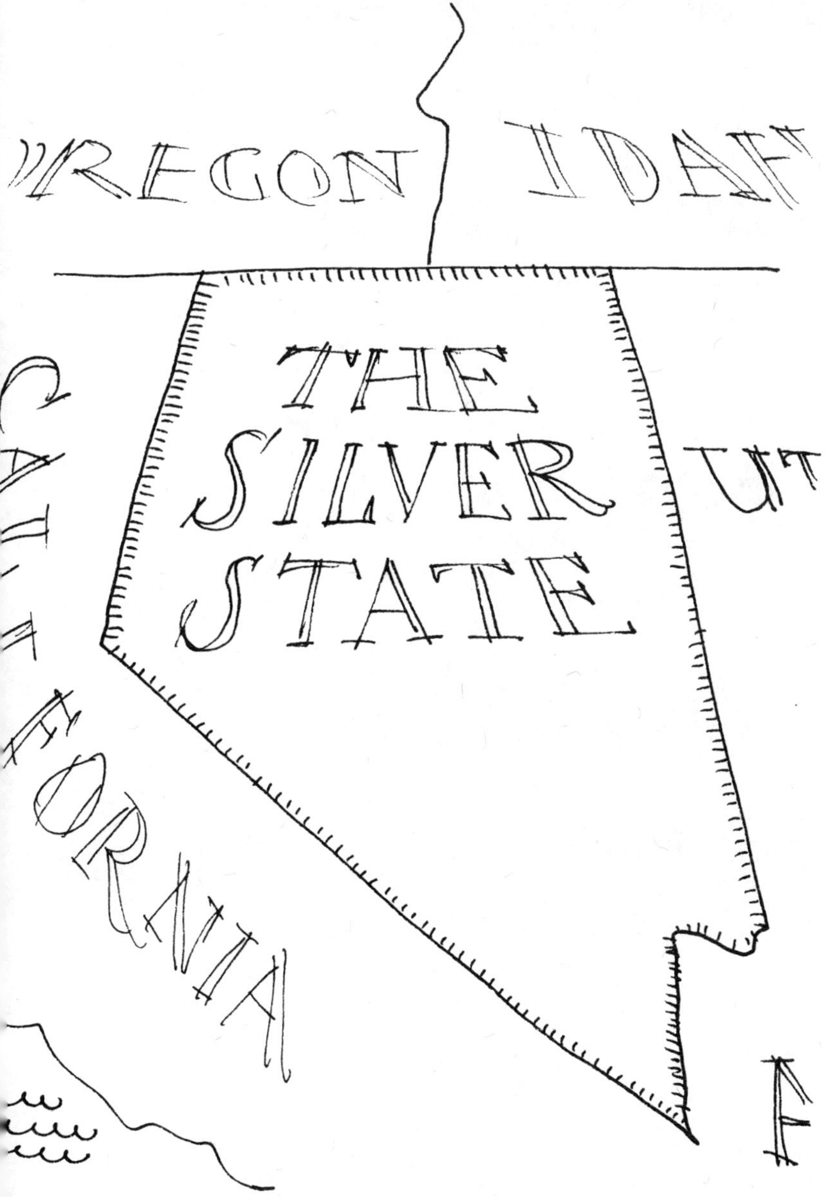

OREGON IDAF

CALIFORNIA

UT

THE
SILVER
STATE

A billion dollars in nickels weighs four times as much, and would fill the skating rink in Radio City to a depth of 24 feet.

And there's enough metal in those nickels to build 16 Eiffel Towers.

no wonder we got such lousy TV!

But when you get
to <u>pennies</u>, the
situation is ridiculous...

A billion dollars in
pennies would weigh
312,500 tons, and

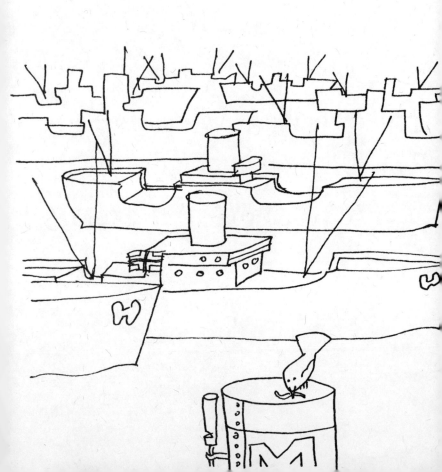

would require a convoy
of 29 C-2 freighters
to carry it.*

* It would also take the government
  20 years to make that many pennies.

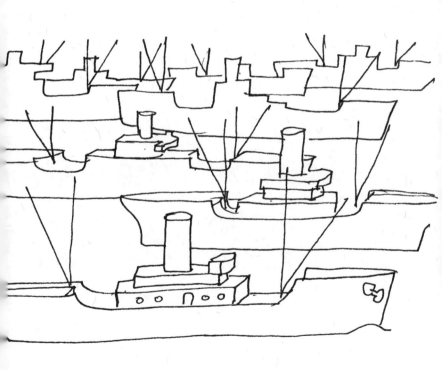

But a billion dollars isn't only big, it has staying power, too. Let's say you had a billion dollars at the sack of Rome (390AD) and you started giving it away at the rate of a dollar a minute every hour of every day. That's $60 an hour, 24 hours a day...

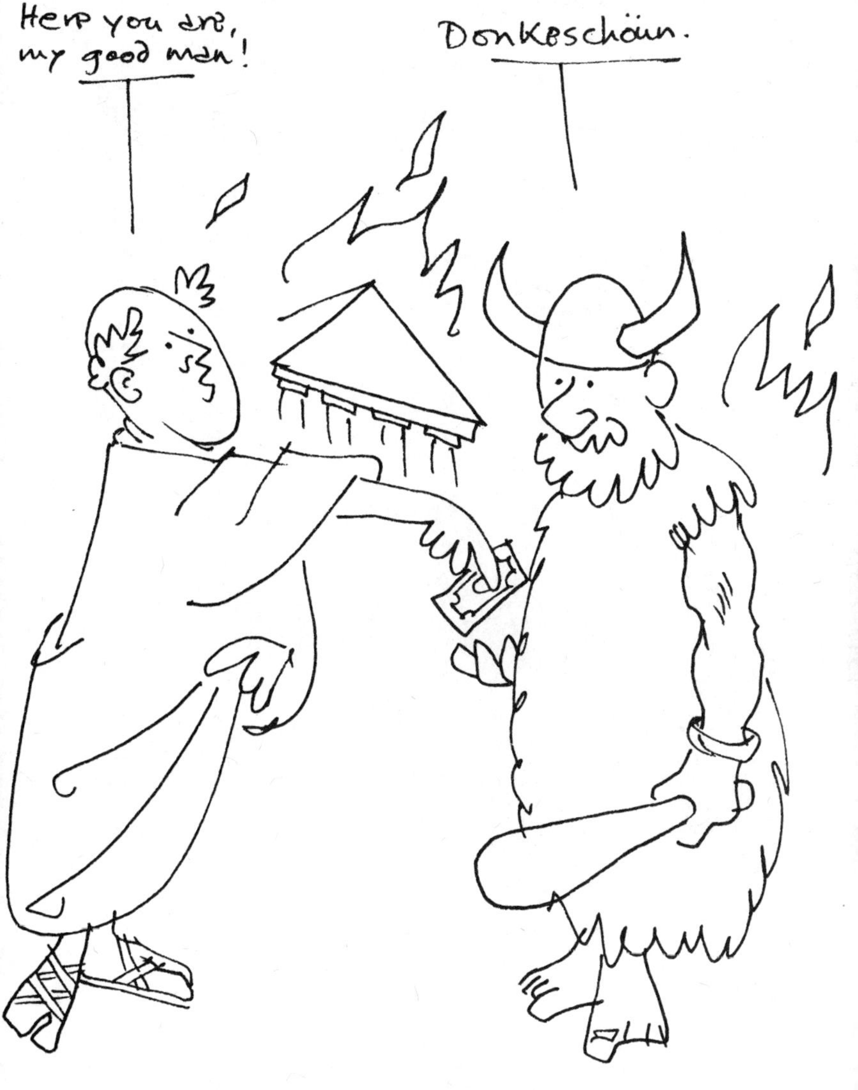
Here you are, my good man!
Donkeschöun.

By Charlemagne's coronation, you would have given away 215 million.

By the Norman Conquest you would have spent 300 million.

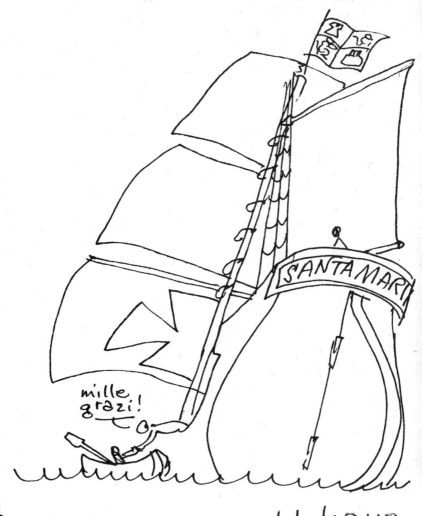

By 1492 you would have
used up almost half
your billion...

And then, as you continued to dole out dollars through the American Revolution...
It hath a pleasing design.
merci beauc...
...the French Revolution...

...the Industrial Revolution...

Gimme!

...and the Russian Revolution,

you could begin to look forward to giving away your last buck...

Yes, a billion
is big.

But it isn't
what it _is_ that's
important.
It's what it
can _buy_...

A billion dollars
could
buy
each
and
every
Rolls-Royce ever built

or, $\frac{1}{5}$ of the
entire U.S.
wheat
crop, or...

...a candy
bar for
everybody
on earth,

HERSHEY'S

?

1978551

just wait
til contract
time...

...or all
24 major
league
baseball
franchises.

A billion dollars would buy effective control of any of these companies:

CBS 👁

Kodak

RCA

Kellogg's

TIME, Inc.

(It could <u>not</u> buy
control of Exxon,
General Motors or
Bell Telephone. Even a
billion has its limits.)

High fliers could bu

fifty fighters, o

three B-1
bombers...

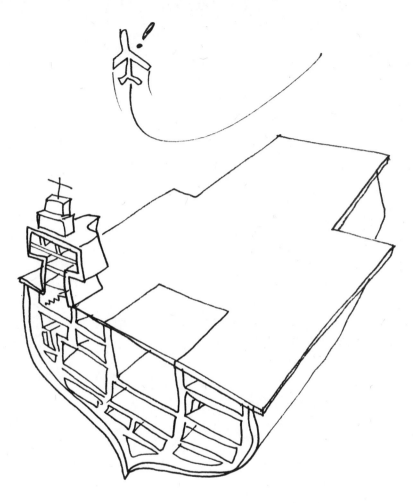

or $\frac{1}{2}$ a "Nimitz" class aircraft carrier.

Why, a billion dollar
could even feed the

United States Government for 19 hours and 21 minutes.

Even when a
billion dollars
isn't doing
anything, it's
doing something...

Put it in a
savings bank, and
it draws interest of...

Looking for a nice
nest egg?

A billion dollars invested in municipal bonds produces

A DOLLAR PER SECOND.

Tax free.

Take this simple test:

I would like to be a billionaire.

☐ YES.

☐ NO.

(check one)

If you answered
"yes," then this
could be your
lucky day,
because...

Look at it
this way:
if you've got a
dollar in your
pocket, you're
already a
BILLIONTHAIRE,
right?
Well, it's a start.

Oh, it won't be easy. Let's say each dot on the opposite page represents a single dollar. You would need 350 THOUSAND pages just like it to show you how many dollars it takes to be a billionaire.

Seems like a lot?
Not really. Remember,
you've got INFLATION
on your side! You
only have to be $\frac{1}{2}$
as lucky, $\frac{1}{2}$ as smart,
$\frac{1}{2}$ as hard-working
as old John D.
Rockefeller to make
your billion!

And let's not hear
how you're too old
to start.

Henry Ford was
broke at 40, and
didn't get started
on _his_ billion
until age 46.

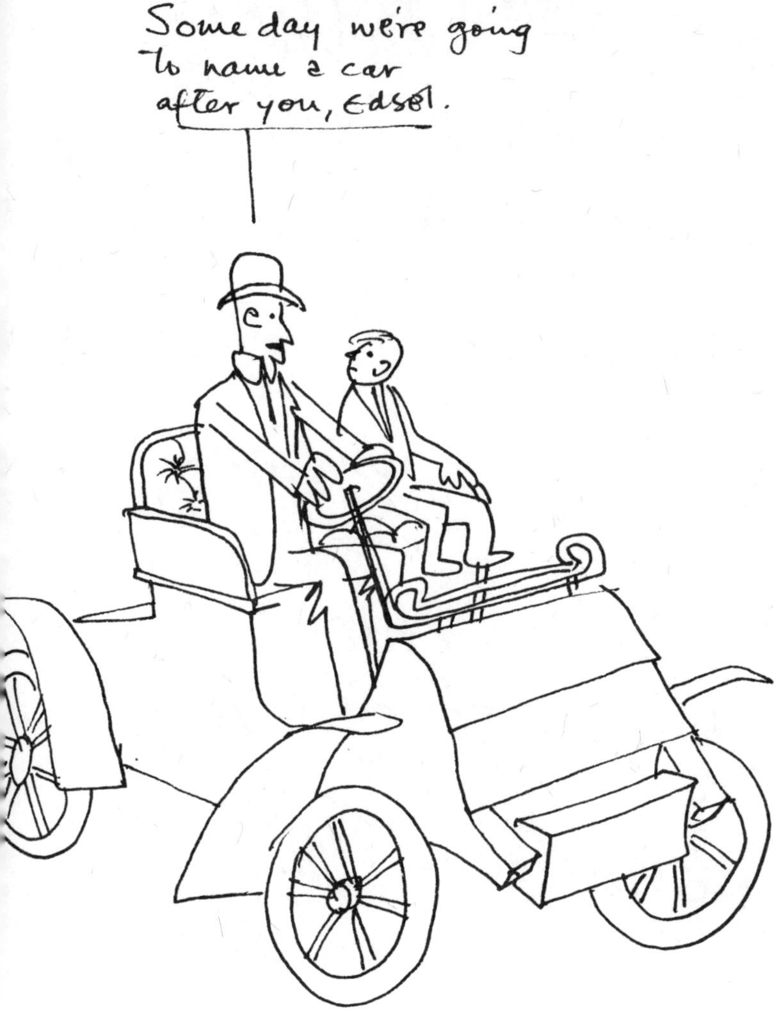
Some day we're going to name a car after you, Edsel.

Best of all, the American billion is the <u>world's</u> <u>smallest</u>.

In most countries a billion has TWELVE zeroes, instead of our nine. So it's easier to make a billion dollars than a billion Deutschmarks or even a billion lira. How lucky can you get

Look, most people are
too busy to notice, but
on an average day there
about $43 billion in
currency floating arou

ut there... why shouldn't 43 of it be yours? Others have made it. Why not you?

Your chances of success are about...

...one in a billion.